AF333521

VANISHING VESTS

ELAYNE REISS-WEIMANN
RITA FRIEDMAN

NEW DIMENSIONS IN EDUCATION, INC.
50 EXECUTIVE BLVD.
ELMSFORD, NY 10523

Printed in U.S.A.

Hardcover ISBN 0-89796-804-2   12131 (Hardcover)
Softcover ISBN 0-89796-221-4   12522 (Softcover)

2 3 4 5 6 7 8 9   SPC   SPC   9 8 7 6 5 4

Valentine's Vest Store is in Valley View.
Mrs. Valentine sells vests of all kinds
to men and women.
There is always a vest in the window.

One morning, Victor, the store manager,
starts to fill customers' orders.
Vera wants a vest for her violin recital.
Velma wants a vest for her ventriloquist act.
Vinnie wants a vest for his volleyball game.
Victor cannot find any vests in his store.
All the vests are gone.
Even the vest in the window has vanished.

Victor calls Virginia's Vest Store.

"Have you seen my vests?" he asks.

"Your vests?" says the salesperson.

"I am looking for my own vests!

All my vests have vanished."

Victor calls vest store after vest store.

Vests have vanished from every store.

RGINIA VEST STORE

The store owners ask their managers
to go to the police station.
"Vests have vanished," they report.
"Vanishing vests?
Very interesting," says the police captain.
"I will call the vest patrol.
They will find the vanishing vests."

The vest patrolmen rush to their cars.

They drive up and down every street.

They call each other on their radios.

"Calling Car One.

Any vanishing vests on your street?

Calling Cars Two, Three, and Four.

Are any vanishing vests to be seen?"

No one can find even one vanishing vest.

V 555
9

Then, suddenly, the vests are seen.
They are walking happily along on a side street.
Car Five stops beside the vests.
"Good day, officers," smile the vests.
"Isn't this a lively morning?"
"It has not been a lovely morning for me,"
says a patrolman.
"Everyone is looking for you."

5

The vests all start to talk at once.

"Please don't say a word!" says the patrolman.

"Just climb into the van."

The vests climb in, and the van races

to the police station.

There, the vests get out of the van.

"Why is everyone angry?" they wonder.

"Today is the day every vest has been waiting for."

The vests are brought before the police captain.
"Vests must not vanish," says the captain.
"Where were you going?"
"Don't you know?" asks the polka dot vest.
"It's really simple," says the striped vest.
"I don't understand," says the captain.
"...But today is the day!"
say all the vests loudly.
"Please tell me what day," pleads the captain.

REPORT

"Today Mr. V visits Valley View,"
says the polka dot vest.
"Mr. V will wear his violet velvet vest!"
"Mr. V?... Violet?... Velvet?... Vest?
I don't understand," says the captain.
All the vests talk at once.
"Today is the day we may see Mr. V and touch his vest.
His vest is velvet.
His vest is violet.
It is very special.
Now Mr. V will not be able to find us."

The police captain listens.
"I am sorry," he says.
"I did not know."
The vest patrolmen listen.
"We are sorry," they say.
"We did not know."
Suddenly, the captain has an idea.
"Get into your patrol cars,"
he says to the vest patrol.
"Ride on every street.
Find Mr. V.
Bring him here."

The patrol cars race away.
The vest patrolmen look for Mr. V.
They look for a violet velvet vest.

4
VV4
3
VV3
2

The vests wait and wait.

"I guess the vest patrol cannot find Mr. V,"
says the striped vest.

Then suddenly, into the police station walks Mr. V.

He is wearing his violet velvet vest!

"He is very special," whisper the vests.

Mr. V smiles.

He walks to the vests.

One by one they touch his violet velvet vest.

They are very happy!

The police captain is happy.
The vest patrol is happy.
They cry tears of happiness.
Mr. V sees the tears.
"You may touch my vest too," he says.
"But first dry your tears.
Tears will spoil my violet velvet vest."

Mr. V cannot stay very long.

He has other vests to visit.

Soon it is time for Mr. V to leave.

Mr. V waves good-bye.

Then Mr. V vanishes.

The vests go back to the shops.
Victor and the other managers
are very happy to see the vests.
The vests are very happy to see them, too.
"We saw Mr. V," they say.
"We touched his violet velvet vest."

The next day all is quiet in Valley View.

The vests are back in the shops.

They do not talk about Mr. V.

But they wonder when Mr. V and his violet velvet vest

will visit again.